Fixing Things

Andrew Aldred

All rights reserved, no part of this publication may be reproduced by any means, electronic, mechanical photocopying, documentary, film or in any other format without prior written permission of the publisher.

>Published by
>Chipmunkapublishing
>United Kingdom

http://www.chipmunkapublishing.com

Copyright © Andrew Aldred

Greenland and the Panama Canal

So, Donald Trump wants to appropriate some territory.
Because that is what Russia and China are trying to do
And yes, the big boys all seem to be at it.
I can see the world being split into three nations.
There will be Russia, China, America and very little else.
Elon Musk seems to want to play politics over here.
Does he really think he is a hero, and everybody likes him?
As Nigel Farage tried to say before Musk withdrew his money
Does Donald Trump think he can walk in and take random territory?
What do Russia and China think of that?
Somewhere along the line people need to be responsible.
Russia needs to stop being aggressive in Eastern Europe
China needs to give up its interest in Taiwan.
North Korea should probably just blow itself up.
And people need to realise things do not need to change.
They were alright before and this is not progress.
End the war in Europe and the Middle East
Can we all get back to normal while we still have a life?

Useless Psychiatrist

What is the point in going to see him?
What use have they been in forty bloody years?
Do they think I need to talk to them?
They gave me some drugs which I take.
They are all I have bloody well got.
To cope with paranoid schizophrenia and psychosis
People are telling lies on the streets.
They do not want to know my point of view.
They see me as less than human.
And I see them as the poison they are.
They bring up their children to be the same.
I cannot be a scapegoat for them.
All they can do is leave me alone.
The useless psychiatrist can see somebody else.

The Masked Singer

This is a very stylised series of programs.
It would appear insane to somebody who has not seen it.
Like a lot of television these days it is an enhanced reality
It is not just people singing, they dress up and we guess who they are.
The television people are so busy putting a different twist on things.
It happens to a lot of programs, take Ninja Warrior or Gladiators
Things used to be a lot simpler in the days of Superstars.
You would watch Geoff Capes and Brian Jacks battle it out.
Have we lost what the shows are about with the new formats?
Is how physically able somebody is or how well they can sing.
Lost in all the elaborate staging and gaudy showbusiness.
I enjoyed the old programs a lot more than the new ones.
They were less elaborate and complicated and more realistic.

Bits of Things

I have been busy all day doing bits of things.
My front wheel on the car needed attention.
I had scraped the alloy on the kerbside.
So, I sanded it down and sprayed it with lacquer.
The weeds in my garden were growing between the paving slabs.
So, I bought a hand-held tool to clean them out.
The oven needed some clips for the thermostat.
Because the ones it came with were broken
So, I ordered them off the internet for next week.
Other things I had ordered needed chasing up because they were late.
So, I did all of this and bought some things from Asda.
It is all bits of things, and I am moving forward slowly.
Tomorrow I will take some goods in for exchange.
At the local music store for some new bass strings
Sooner or later, everything will be to rights again.
And I will be able to move on to larger projects again.

Poorly Partner

I have been everywhere with Jane about her problems.
To the doctors, the hospital, the health centre and the chemist
She suffers from a variety of health problems that affect her mobility.
We both wish she could be better, and this was not the case.
Life is such a struggle and all she can do is take painkillers.
She would love to be able to go shopping in town.
But everything we used to do now requires a wheelchair.
Both our mothers had mobility problems later in life
It is frightening not knowing how things will be from day to day.
Whether she will be able to do the housework or cook a meal
The doctor has given us a plan and I hope it works.
Because if it does not, I do not know what we will do.
Life is all too short and full of problems as we grow older.

Fixing a Table

Jane gave me an old table yesterday.
And I was going to take it to the tip.
Before I had the idea to fix it
It had four bits of wood in the corners.
That had seen much better days.
So, I knocked them out with a mallet.
And went on the internet for some brackets.
Which I put in with thirty-two screws
Then I secured it with some glue
I was able to fix a table today.

Everything is Late

Royal Mail is providing a hopeless service.
Everything is late or lost in the post.
Takeover by a Czech billionaire has done no good
I am left waiting for things that should have arrived.
But the Post Office boys are on a go slow.
They have given up trying to squeeze the company.
For more money and now they will not work
I know Christmas is the busiest time of the year.
And half the world is down with the flu.
But please do your job is what I would say to you.
Second class mail should not take ten days.
Before it is delivered to your doorstep
What has happened to you all recently?
If you want to rest your head in bed
You will be short of money and in the red.
Please sort yourselves out because I doubt.
Whether Royal Mail is reliable or viable any more

Mending the Cooker

The clips for the thermostat had perished.
On my twenty-year-old Prestige cooker
So, I ordered some off eBay on the internet.
And with difficulty I fixed the thermostat
Then I noticed the door lining had perished
So, I got door seal and glue off Amazon.
And a new set of knobs for the controls
I got oven cleaner from the supermarket.
And with luck this oven will last another ten years
So, I will not have to buy a new one soon.
And get it plumbed in when the old one is gone.

More Money

More money is all anyone wants these days.
The foreign holidays and fancy car giveaways
Every time food, electrical goods or the mortgage goes up.
They all want to go on strike and ask for more wages.
And they wonder why this country is falling to pieces.
Why there are potholes on every street and things are in disrepair.
It is because they want more money, and they do not care.
Nobody wants to economise or make do and mend.
They want the latest of everything and they want it now.
And they think because they are in work, they should have it.
The Labour government wants to renew everything and grow the economy.
But I am afraid all of that is down to you and me.
We all have to do without for the things our country needs.
Everyone is already looking to Nigel Farage to take over.
But you know what he is like from his drinking habits.
You could have a good discussion with him in a pub.
But is he really fit for this country's highest office?
People do not need more money; they need to do more.
In terms of looking after their bodies and property and spending less

Soul in Torment

The boy on the TV is a little over seventeen.
And has committed three murders and injured many.
He is proud and unrepentant for what he has done.
But the picture on the TV is like a Halloween mask.
A very damaged boy who only knows how to hate
And you can only imagine whatever has gone wrong.
His face will be in my memory for a very long time.
They gave him fifty-two years for the Southport killings.
But he has already died and gone to hell.
He will forever be a soul in torment locked in a cell.
And he simply does not understand the pain he has caused.

Poorly Partner

She has had severe problems with her mobility.
For over three months now and we cannot see an end
To her suffering with pain in her back and her legs
All we get is ever more medication to kill the pain.
But no lasting solution to her agonising problems
Myalgia and degenerative changes to the lumbar spine
Are the diagnoses but she is not getting better?
We are both living with this very limiting problem.
And we both desperately hope she will get a little better.
I am staying over almost every night of the week.
And trying to do the things she used to be able to
The cat does not understand what the matter is.
And we are so tired of keeping on keeping on.
All we have is our love and a hope that things will improve.

Drugs and Alcohol?

Drugs and alcohol have never mixed very well.
In short you cannot take both in excess
You should really ditch the tablets or the alcohol.
You might need both or you might think you do.
But you really will have to settle for one or the other.
Drugs and alcohol are a lethal combination and have killed many.
If your medical condition dictates that you need medication
You should probably take what you are prescribed and not drink.
We ditched alcohol a long time ago, but we need medication.

You are all Mad

You think I am a drug addict.
You think I have a bizarre sex life.
You think I am swindling the state.
You think this and you think that.
Because that is where you are all at
You would not know normality if it hit you.
Because you are all freaks and perverts
All I want is to be left alone with my partner.
To carry on what life we have got together.
People hate me but it is a sad reflection on them.
Does everybody really think they are less crazy than me?
You are all mad and most of you need locking up.
But they do not even want you in prison.
Because you are too disruptive and never knew any better

So Perfect, So Bland

Artificial intelligence is fast taking over everything.
There will be no more real literature or music.
I am buying up everything I can from the past.
Because it will not be here in another five years
It will be replaced by a load of computerised crap.
You will be buying a book by a computer instead of me.
You could write a song on a computer thirty years ago.
And people might as well be lip syncing everything.
Because they are not allowed to do things for real any more
Every gig you ever went to is just a soundtrack.
The stars do a bit of talking, dancing and lip syncing.
What on earth is the point in going to see that?
If I buy something I want it to be authentic and real
I want it to be played, sung and written by people.
They have killed our creative industries with computers.
Everything that was ever good is now in the past.

You Got What You Wanted

The American people have got the president they wanted.
Donald Trump is sitting for another term of office.
He will make America great again and we will pay for it.
Nobody seems to care what is right as long as there is more money.
I do not care what people say but the world has gone to the dogs.
Do people want to fight and die for Donald Trump's America?
Well, count me out, I preferred Kamala Harris
And America can have its new version of Uncle Sam
I only hope you are able to vote him out in four years.
You got what you wanted and confirmed our fears.

No Good to Me

Do I want extra runways at every airport?
Do I want a new stadium at Manchester United?
I hate to say it, but the answer is no.
Labour is busy wasting my money.
I will not be going on a foreign holiday.
I am not interested in going to watch football.
Are these really what economic growth means?
Is this really where we get our revenue?
Do we not export anything to the world anymore?
I agree we need a lot of extra homes.
And we are going to need the immigrants coming in.
Because our population is getting too old to work
We need the immigrants and the housing.
All they talk about is smashing people smuggling gangs.
Building new football stadiums and airports
The Labour government is bloody crazy.
And their policies are no good to me.

Not Fit for Purpose

The police and the mental health service
Are not helping me at all with my problems.
They think it is me that is not fit for purpose.
But I am bloody sure it is them.
They give me medication but that is all.
They made me jump through endless hoops.
For forty years while I suffered
I asked the doctor to be discharged today.
What did I ever need them for anyway?
All they did was make my problems worse.
Medication with bad side effects did not help.
Years of being in mental hospital made me no better
I get my benefits and my army pension.
I now no longer need the mental health service.
All they did was take the piss out of me for years.
So, I am not fit for purpose, and neither are they?
The community can be as unhappy as they like.
Everybody should have just left me alone.
Things would have worked out a lot better.
What were they trying to teach me anyway?
Only that they hate me and are full of shit.
Everybody is the same as they ever were.
I will carry on being me and they will carry on being them.

Opportunist

Trump wants to take possession of Gaza.
He wants to repatriate all Palestinians.
He does not care about the ethics of this.
He just wants to make a profit out of a catastrophe.
He has a background in property development.
All of this is an opportunity to make money.
Israel has fought a war on his behalf.
And he will clean up the mess for a price.
He will make America great again at your expense.
He has never cared what is right or wrong.
All he cares about is America and its bank balance.

Robot Counsellor

They want you to tell your problems to your phone.
They want you to talk to the chatbot at your bank.
The last thing they want you to do is think for yourself.
We are all looking for an answer to our problems.
We are all looking for a needle in a very large haystack.
But we should all be thinking for ourselves about our situation.
If you need a robot to help you out there is something wrong
They are getting information about you all the time.
But nobody knows your situation better than you.
So why don't you make the decisions and sack the robot.

Decorating Her Bedroom

Her bedroom is the largest room in her house.
I started by getting the mirror off the wall.
Then I bought some paint the same colour
As some paint, we already had and kept.
She had removed some of the wallpaper.
And I went round the room removing furniture.
And stripping the wall with water and a scraper
When it was all done, I started painting.
Being careful not to tread paint into the carpet
And cleaning up every day after I had finished.
After ten days the room is practically done
There is a little bit behind some shelves to paint.
Then I can breathe easy until my next project
I have evaded decorating this room for years.
But very soon it will be finished in a shade of pink.

Angry and Bitter

All the psychiatric services have done for me.
Is make me progressively more ill.
And make me feel angry and bitter about them.
A system that is based on rape, torture and abuse
Will never be any good to the people it serves.
And I am talking about the patients, not the public.
They always whip the media up into a frenzy.
Whenever psychiatric illness and crime are mentioned.
But society should think about what it has done to these people.
To make them do desperately violent and crazy crimes.
Do they even consider the way the mentally ill are treated?
We are all trying to uphold a system that is rotten.
The people we listen to are corrupt and misguided.
I am living in a society I do not believe in
And all I can do is feel angry and bitter about it.

Status Quo

Donald Trump and Vladimir Putin had a phone call.
They discussed the future of Ukraine.
With nobody else present or involved
Europe is being frozen out of the peace talks.
The Ukrainian president has not been called in.
So how the fuck is this going to work at all?
Mess around with the status quo and it changes.
And you risk it never being the same as it was.
Peace would be a wonderful thing for everybody.
If we could go back to some form of stability
If we had some consensus and economic security
So, what are Trump and Putin really up to?
We will all have to wait to find that out.
But the status quo will never be the same again.

Psychopaths

The world is full of them, and they are mostly in charge.
Donald Trump, Elon Musk, Vladimir Putin to name a few.
People who have radical ideas and a lot of self-belief
People who follow no rules and have no rationale.
Look at what Benjamin Netanyahu has done to Gaza.
And what Trump has proposed to clean up the mess?
The unthinkable is happening before our eyes.
And you are always left wondering what will come next.
Trump is talking about changing the American constitution.
And that is what the American people mostly seem to want.
Sooner or later a lot of people will get very upset.
And they will turn around and declare what is right.
There may be war and confrontation on a wide scale.
When the people have had enough, they will blame the leaders.
When you are in charge of a nation you have to take responsibility
And when you fall from grace it is a hell of a drop
If the people in charge do not start getting things right
Pretty soon everything is going to start going wrong.

Peace

Peace would be a wonderful thing right now.
Peace in Europe, Israel and Lebanon
But I do not know how anyone will bring that about.
Could Trump and Putin ever do anything good?
I really doubt it and I think we are all being played.
If that was not the case, we would be involved.
We are all wanting to know what happens.
Peace would be great, but it will come at a cost.

Deal or No Deal

Donald Trump has talked to a lot of leaders.
First Putin, then Macron, Starmer and Zelensky
But everything has stumbled at the last hurdle.
Zelensky has walked out without a deal.
And everything is in a state of turmoil once again.
America has bills to pay like everybody else.
And Zelensky and Ukraine have leaned heavily on everyone.
World peace will always come at a cost.
You can hate somebody as much as you like.
But you should respect his point of view and hear him out.
It is a case of as long as the price is right.
But Donald Trump has sold Ukraine down the river.
Russian soldiers are on the horizon.
Ukrainians need to salvage what they can of their nation.
Zelensky has been more than a hero to many.
But he has been ambushed and is unable to secure peace.
And this is not the outcome many had hoped for.
I guess its no deal for now. Watch this space.

Cycle of Abuse

It has to end somewhere and now is the time.
I am getting abused in the community and by mental health services.
In order to supposedly make me better
Well, I have news for you. I am as well as I can be.
I want to be discharged as soon as possible.
I am a respectable ex-soldier, and I am retired.
So why do you not see fit to leave me alone.
All I want to do is be able to get on.
I have learned everything the psychiatrist can teach me.
It is time for me to get on and do my own thing.
I really do not care who is happy and who is not.
I am fifty-nine years old, and it is my life.
Time to end this cycle of abuse for everyone.

Awkward Situation

Trump has set out his stall very clearly.
He does not want to fight Putin's Russia
He wants the war in Ukraine to end very soon.
And he wants the rights to Ukraine's minerals.
Starmer seems to think he can win Trump over.
But ourselves and our willing partners are not enough.
And we will not commit to an all-out war.
Zelensky is holding out for a fair deal for Ukraine.
And I am in some doubt as to whether that will happen.
Trump is already blaming him for a third world war.
Is he supposed to just let them carve up his country?
Russia is waiting to take advantage in the sidelines.
Of a country that cannot fight on forever
A United States that will not defend democracy.
And a NATO that is fractured and dysfunctional
It is an awkward situation and there is no clear solution.
Zelensky will not bow down to Trump and Putin
We are not going to take on Russia by ourselves.
And somehow, we have to unpick this mess.
This will involve all parties sitting around a table.
Where most are uneasy and do not want to be involved
Could our leaders ever come to a compromise?
Could Zelensky, Trump, Putin, Macron and Starmer ever agree?
And talk constructively about what they are going to do?
This needs to happen to sort out an awkward situation.

Not Getting Better

I have a forty-year-old mental illness.
Where I have been raped at night
While I am lying in my bed asleep
It will not just go away.
And I will be living with it forever.
They cannot wipe my memory clean.
I have numerous physical health problems.
But I do not need any operations.
And the doctors cannot force them on me.
I detest the mental illness I have had.
They cannot repair a worn-out body.
And they cannot change my mind.
I am as well as I can be and will get no better
I will be sixty next year. It is time to wind it down.

Every Man for Himself

The public seem to want something back.
For the money I get for my illness
They want to perpetuate it and see me suffer.
But I really cannot give them anything.
The next-door neighbours want me to leave.
But I have to live somewhere and will not move.
My partner and I are too ill to work.
All we can do is keep out of sight and carry on.
China seems to want to have a pop at America.
America does not want to help us with nuclear arms.
Ukraine seems to be left in the lurch by everyone.
Gaza has to do what they are told or die.
It is a dog-eat-dog world that is getting worse.
You cannot believe what is on TV anymore.
Artificial Intelligence means nobody knows what to believe.
It is every man for themselves in a very dangerous world.

Social Media Scammers

Why does anybody use social media?
All it does is take your money.
You can give to any number of causes.
You can get impersonated and ripped off.
They are making money out of you.
Keep your information to yourself.
And be careful what you do on your phone.
Because you will lose money everywhere
And you need what you get for yourself.
There are more scammers than real people.
On social media and the internet now

Sacrifice

My brother has looked after my father.
Ever since our mother passed away.
I have been busy taking care of things.
For my partner over her mother's death and estate
I have never looked for any financial reward.
But my brother does not make a lot of money.
He works for the council picking up litter.
He needs somewhere to live with his wife.
So, my father is rewriting his will.
To try to give my brother a better share
So, his future will be secure, and he will have a house.
For my part I do not need the money
I do not want to have to sort out my father's affairs.
My brother does not want much to do with me.
And has a life of his own down in Wales.
I nearly killed my father twenty-eight years ago.
And I am prepared to make this sacrifice.
To try to ensure my brother has a future.

An Ill Wind

There is an ill wind blowing at the moment.
Too many big chiefs banging their drums.
Too many angry people unable to listen.
To what their enemies think and feel
There has to be a will to sort things out.
There are too many people suffering.
Most of us want to live and be happy.
We are all tired of the misery and hardship.
And yet it seems to go on and on
It is an ill wind that blows nobody any good
There has to be a change for the better
To end the wars and heal the nations again.

Guilty?

People are sitting back to see what will happen.
The mental health services want nothing to do with me.
I am busy getting on with my life the best way I can.
I am not sure the family I had want to know me.
Sooner or later, this will all be boxed up and thrown away.
And maybe I can sleep at night and have my life back.
Anyone who thinks I am some sort of Jesus is wrong.
But I am certainly not the devil or any other God.
I am just a very average man who has had a difficult life.
All I want is to be retired and left with my partner.
After everything that has happened it is not too much to ask
People are still trying to pin something on me after forty years.
And it is time they realised that they are the guilty ones.

The Same Place

This world could be heaven or hell.
But that only depends on your outlook.
Is the glass half empty or half full?
Can you be happy with yourself or not?
I have always made the best of a bad job.
I have always been able to get along with things.
I am not a bitter man and can actually be happy.
I will not be chasing money until I am in a grave.
I have peace of mind and a clear conscience.
There are people who envy me and those that do not.
Leave the hating to those who are stupid and ignorant.
It will always come back and get them in the end.
Heaven and hell are exactly the same place.
It just depends on how you view them.

Admit it.

Psychiatric services are supposed to help people.
But they have helped everyone else instead.
And they have left me in an impossible situation.
I cannot alter myself to other people's specifications.
I will only be myself whatever other people think or do.
So maybe it is time for them to think again?
They have had it all their own way and it has not worked.
Psychiatric services are no use to me anymore.
I need the police and medical profession to take me seriously.
Everybody else is to blame for their own madness.
If psychiatric services are no use to me, they should admit it.
And stop giving me extra hoops to jump through to get better.

Illness

I have had a virus recently.
It has impacted my mental and physical health.
I had cancer of the larynx ten years ago.
I am having difficulty talking and swallowing.
I have been to the hospital to see the doctor.
They sent me to have a barium meal.
And although there is nothing wrong further down
There is something wrong with my larynx.
But this time it is not getting any worse
The discoloration is getting smaller.
And the chances are that I will recover.
I have to take things at a slower pace now.
I am not as ironclad as I was.
I am now a paid carer for Jane.
And I will have to be well to do that.

Grind to a Halt

President Trump is trying to end the wars.
And it is commendable that he believes in peace.
But it will take a lot to bring it about
He holds the cards, and we have to put faith in him.
And hope he provides a solution for everyone.
And America and everyone else can be great again.
It has been a stand off in Ukraine and Gaza
And everything is beginning to grind to a halt.
The Russians are trying to take back their own territory.
And the Israelis are trying to get back the hostages.
These bitter wars have lasted long enough.
It is time to reset again and return to normality.
Everything needs rebuilding again.
Everybody is exhausted and needs their life back.
Things are going to grind to a halt.
And let's hope there is a lasting solution to the problems.

Is Mental Illness Real?

Mental illness is very real to those suffering it.
I have lived too long and been through too much.
For anyone to believe I am some sort of fake person
You can laugh your head off at me it you want.
But you must realise I value what I have and the life I have got.
And things could be a hell of a lot worse for me.
I take my tablets and will remain mentally ill forever.
Because that is what the doctor has said I need to do
I follow the rules like anyone with any sense would.
There is a purpose to society and the structure of it.
We all have to go through a lot to get paid.
And I am no different to anyone else in that respect.
I am a good mentally ill person so please try to see it that way.
I have very little choice in the matter and am not in charge.

Better Times and Brighter Days

It is spring and the sun is beginning to shine.
Another winter over and soon I will be in the garden again.
I am getting out for a walk with my partner Jane.
And we are picking ourselves up after a winter of illness.
Hopefully the world situation will begin to sort out.
Nobody wants a third world war, and it is not in our interests.
America can be great and prosperous while we all get forgotten.
It is another year; we are still alive, and things will be better.

Rogue Nations

You did not believe Trump when he talked about Canada.
He said jokingly that it was America's fifty first state.
You did not believe him when he talked about the Panama Canal
And you probably did not believe him when he talked about Greenland.
He has also made a plan of what he wants to do with the Gaza strip.
You think he is insane, but you come to realise he is serious.
First Russia took Crimea and now they are carving up Ukraine.
Trump and Putin are playing games with the world's territories.
Individual countries are too weak to withstand the superpowers.
NATO and the UN are not credible organisations anymore.
Rogue nations are beginning to carve up the world as we know it.

Getting on Without America

Russia and Ukraine seem content to continue fighting.
So do Israel and Gaza and nobody listens to America.
People are intent on doing their own thing without the USA.
If America wants to dictate everything it will end up excluded
Donald Trump's ideas seem to be backfiring on him.
Everybody seems to be sick of being told what to do.
And if America does not co-operate, we will find new friends.
China has said it is up for a war of any kind with America.
And all of us "little people" seem to be finding our own way.

Mental Health Services

They have not been to visit for ten months.
I explained that I did not need them by phone.
They are never there when required and complicate things.
I need their medication, but I do not need them.
How can they give me advice after a forty-year illness?
Everything that could happen has done at least once.
The worker I spoke to has to talk to the psychiatrist.
But very soon I will be rid of mental health services.
Everybody has lived off my mental illness for long enough.
Please find someone else who desperately needs help.
And I sincerely hope you do a better job for them.
I have lived through forty years of this shit.
And I am not worth much to anyone except Jane.

Fix Yourselves

People seem to like to see me as the enemy.
They all want to take something out on me.
But I am not here to mend other people's grievances.
None of you will fix yourselves by breaking me.
People need to look to themselves to see what is wrong.
And then they need to put it right in a way
That satisfies them and leaves me alone.
God knows what I have done to be judged so guilty.
But I am not tortured by my conscience about anything.
If everyone else could live with themselves, it would be better.
Make this world right for yourselves and let me get on.
If you are broken, fix yourselves and like me you will be happy.

School Shooter

He murdered his mother, sister and brother.
Then he went to school to kill them
All he wanted was to be notorious.
To be known as the worst of the worst
He was fixated with extreme violence.
Why did he ever exist in this world?
What on earth is the point in people like him?
Will forty-nine years in prison be enough?
Some people choose to be like him, others do not.
Thank God I have something and someone to live for
Everyone starts off with a blank slate.
Sometimes choices get made for them that are wrong.
But ultimately people make their own choices.
And this young man has made some very bad ones.

Crazy Kid

When I look back thirty or so years
I was just a crazy kid trying to survive.
And I have not really changed that much.
I am older, weaker and wiser to a large extent.
I was put in a corner, and I fought my way out.
I pleaded guilty and took the consequences.
If it happened again, I would plead innocence.
I would somehow have got rid of this madness.
And got on with my life better than I have.
I have given them all someone to pick on.
For a long time but I am not the guilty one
I used to be a victim, but I turned that around.
My illness might be worth something to you.
You can learn from my mistakes and experience.
But it really has no value whatsoever to me

www.ingramcontent.com/pod-product-compliance
Lightning Source LLC
Chambersburg PA
CBHW031553210526
45464CB00003B/1288